KT-151-630

Forest

DK

LONDON, NEW YORK, MUNICH,
MELBOURNE, and DELHI

Written and edited by Deborah Lock
and Lorrie Mack
Designed by Janet Allis

Publishing manager Sue Leonard
Managing art editor Clare Shedden
Jacket design Chris Drew
Picture researcher Jo de Gray and
Sarah Stewart-Richardson
Production Shivani Pandey
DTP Designer Almudena Díaz
Consultant Samantha Sawyer

First published in Great Britain in 2004 by
Dorling Kindersley Limited
80 Strand, London WC2R 0RL

2 4 6 8 10 9 7 6 5 3 1

A Penguin Company
Copyright © 2004 Dorling Kindersley Limited, London

A CIP catalogue record for this book
is available from the British Library.

All rights reserved. No part of this publication may be
reproduced, stored in a retrieval system, or transmitted
in any form or by any means, electronic, mechanical,
photocopying, recording, or otherwise, without the prior
written permission of the copyright owner.

ISBN 1-4053-0091-4

Colour reproduction by Colourscan, Singapore
Printed and bound in Italy by LEGO

See our complete catalogue at
www.dk.com

Contents

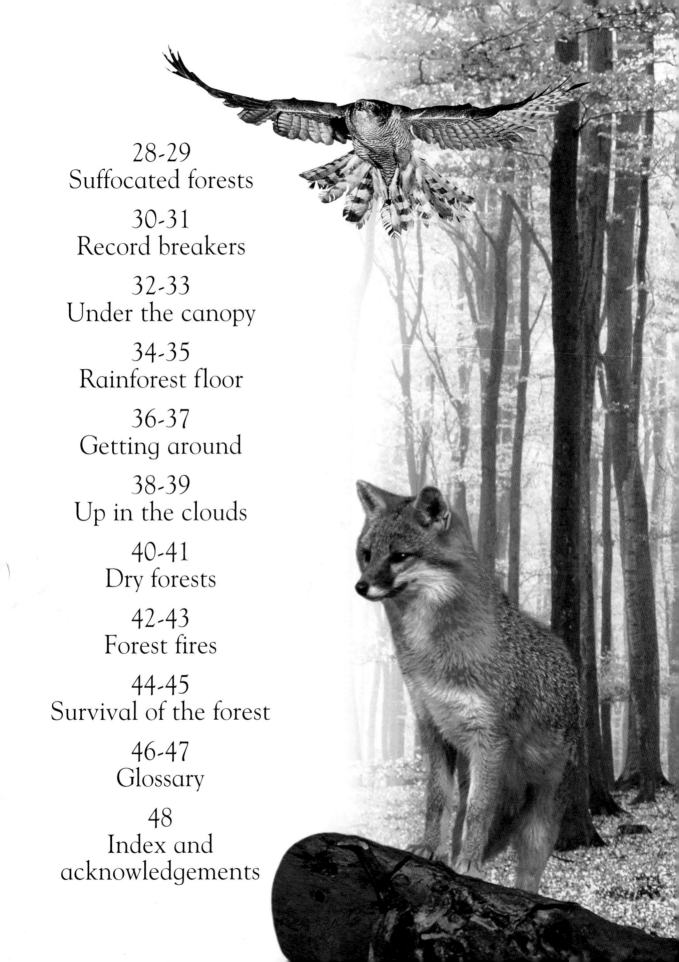

Forest features

Using water, carbon dioxide from the air, and sunlight, leaves produce food for the tree. This process is called photosynthesis.

A large area of trees clumped together is called a forest. However, a forest is much more than this. Step inside and you'll discover a wide variety of plants, with lots of different animals living among them.

Parts of a tree

The trunk of the tree supports the crown of branches, which bear leaves, flowers, fruits, or cones. The roots anchor the tree into the ground and soak up goodness from the soil.

These new leaves are shaped like those on the fully-grown tree.

Flowers produce seeds from which new trees can grow.

The bark protects the wood that carries goodness between the branches and the roots.

Birth of a tree

Most seeds are eaten, or trampled on, or fall in places where they cannot grow. If a seed survives, its case cracks open. Roots break through, then a stem appears above the ground, and finally the first leaves unfold.

A fallen tree is home to animals, such as woodlice and millipedes, feeding on the rotting wood.

The roots spread out sideways and downwards, soaking up water and minerals.

A barn owl hunts small animals, such as the shrew.

The forest community

A forest is a massive food web. Parts of living and rotting plants are eaten by many tiny animals, which are eaten by other animals that are hunted by other animals. Changes can affect the balance of the whole community.

A shrew looks for insects to eat.

An oak moth caterpillar eats the leaves of an oak tree.

Where in the world?

autumn   *summer*

winter   *spring*

Almost a third of all the land on Earth is covered by trees. In different parts of the world, the climate and the altitude affect the types of tree that can grow. There are three main types of forest – deciduous forest, coniferous forest, and rainforest.

Changing seasons

In some regions, temperature and rainfall change dramatically through the year, so all living things have to adapt. This tree is divided into four sections that show how the branches look in autumn, winter, spring, and summer.

Find your forest

In cold places, forests are usually coniferous. Rainforests grow in hot, damp climates. Areas that are sometimes warm and sometimes cool are called temperate zones. These are where temperate, or deciduous, forests are found.

Coniferous forests

Deciduous forests

NORTH AMERICA

Equator

Rainforests

SOUTH AMERI

Deciduous forests

Trees that shed their leaves in autumn and grow new ones in spring are known as deciduous. It is never very hot or very cold in these deciduous, or temperate, forests.

Forest words

Altitude The height a place or region is situated above the level of the sea.

Climate The average weather of an area in terms of temperature, rain, wind, etc.

Equator An imaginary circle around the middle of the Earth where the weather is hot all year round.

Coniferous forests

Where conditions are cool and harsh, trees grow hard, permanent needles for protection instead of leaves that fall off. They also have tough cones in place of flowers to hold their seeds. This type of tree is called coniferous, or evergreen.

Coniferous forests

Deciduous forests

EUROPE

ASIA

AFRICA

Rainforests

Rainforests

AUSTRALIA

Rainforests

Usually found in tropical regions, dense, jungly rainforests grow where the climate is always warm and wet. Although these forests cover only seven per cent of the land in the world, more than half of all existing plant and animal species live in them.

Tree story

There have been plants of some kind on Earth for 420 million years, but the first forests were full of tall ferns rather than trees. It wasn't until about 210 million years ago that forests began to look like the ones we know today.

Disappearing forests

For thousands of years, people have depended on trees. At the same time, they have destroyed vast expanses of precious woodland.

Historical rings

Scientists learn a great deal about trees by examining the rings inside their trunks – each ring indicates one year of growth. A wide ring shows that the tree grew quickly that year; a narrow ring means a year when growth was slow.

At one time, Robin Hood's Sherwood Forest covered over 405 sq km (100,000 acres). Today, it is a 2-sq-km (500-acre) nature reserve.

The outer layer of bark is made up of dead cells that also hold clues to the tree's past life.

Relics of the past

When trees live in damp earth, they are sometimes preserved permanently by minerals in the water. These fossils, called petrified trees, tell us what forests were like millions of years ago.

The oldest wood is at the centre of the tree. It is composed mainly of dead cells. This old, hard wood is called heartwood.

Changing forests

After the era of ferny plantlife, tropical rainforests dominated our planet, which was once warmer than it is now. Later, temperate and evergreen woods spread across lands that were not near the Equator.

TOOLS OF DESTRUCTION

Huge areas of early forest were destroyed by the Vikings, a warlike people who lived in northern Europe hundreds of years ago. Vikings thrived because they were good at metalwork, so they could make sharp axes to cut down trees. The wood was used to build houses and ships, then the cleared land was planted with crops.

Dinosaurs roamed freely in prehistoric forests. Stegosaurus, who lived between 206 and 144 million years ago, ate easy-to-reach plant snacks, such as ferns and seed cones.

Awakening forest

Most trees and plants in the deciduous forest come to life in the spring, when the days get longer and the Sun begins to warm the earth. At this time, birds start building nests and baby animals are born.

New life

Even in winter, the trees are dotted with buds. These are covered with hard scales to protect the tiny new flowers, leaves, and stems inside from the cold.

In the light and warmth of the Sun, this horse chestnut bud bursts open.

Wake-up call

Prickly hedgehogs burrow underground when the cold weather comes. They stay there sleeping until springtime, then crawl out and start looking around for food.

Safe home

Huddled safely in a nest made from twigs and leaves, these bullfinch chicks are being fed by their father. His bright pink breast makes him easy to identify.

Babe in the woods

Red deer live mostly in wooded places. Their young have spotted coats that blend into the speckly light filtering through the trees. This camouflage makes it harder for predators to find them.

Flowering forest

Before the tall trees get covered with leaves, lots of sun can get through, so bluebells, foxgloves, and other wild flowers carpet the forest in springtime.

Life in the trees

A single tree in a forest can be a home, a food source, or a shelter for a variety of animals. Often hidden from view, there is a world of wildlife activity.

Tree dwellers

High up in the trees, squirrels' nests, called dreys, can be found hidden among the branches. After scurrying down to the ground to find fruits and stored nuts, squirrels return there to rest.

The grey squirrel uses its bushy tail to balance as it runs about, and twitches it to communicate with other squirrels.

Insect farmers

Aphids feed on the sap of plants. They produce a sticky liquid called honeydew that ants eat. Often ants can be seen rubbing the aphids to squeeze out the honeydew. In return, ants protect the aphids from enemies.

Searchers

After using its pointed beak to peck through the bark, a green woodpecker can reach into the tree with its long, sticky tongue to lick up any hidden insect larvae.

Ivy is an evergreen plant that uses a tree as a support to climb up towards the sunlight.

Burrowers

The tangled web of a tree's roots provides an ideal place for badgers to dig out their home, called a sett. Usually, this has a number of entrance holes and sleeping chambers with underground tunnels linking them together.

Forest facts

- Green woodpeckers prefer ants and can eat 2,000 a day.
- When badgers leave their setts, foxes or rabbits often come to live there.
- Some beetles lay their eggs within the bark of a tree. When the larvae hatch out, they are near their food.

Rich pickings

Forest plants and animals help each other. For example, some animals eat berries and nuts, while others help to fertilize plants by taking pollen from one flower to another. Sometimes, animals carry seeds to where they have plenty of space, light, and food to grow.

Sweet nectar

When insects land on flowers to drink the nectar, powdery pollen sticks to their legs and bodies. As they move on, the pollen goes with them to fertilize the next flower.

Pollen clings to bees' furry bodies.

Fruity flowers

Once they've been fertilized, flowers turn into fruit or nuts. These contain the seeds that will become new plants.

Forest facts

● Most fleshy fruits, such as berries, contain lots of seeds. Nuts are hard, dry fruits with just one seed inside.

● Each seed has a baby plant and a supply of food enclosed inside a hard case.

● Flowers have bright petals and strong, sweet scents to attract insects.

Nutty name

Nuthatches get their name from the nuts they eat. They have very strong beaks so they can get inside tough shells easily.

Buried treasure
Chipmunks bury acorns in the earth, so they'll have food for the winter. Often, they forget what they've done, and the acorns grow into oak trees!

Hitching a ride
Some seeds are stored inside sticky burrs that get caught on animal fur. Eventually, they fall off, and some of them land on fertile ground.

Feasting for winter
This American black bear is filling up on woodland berries. During the autumn, he needs to eat as much as he can to keep him going through the long, cold winter.

Falling leaves

In the autumn, the forest floor becomes littered with the multi-coloured leaves that have fallen off the trees. Many creepy-crawlies feed on the rotting leaves, while other animals feast on these tiny animals.

Colour changes

Leaves get their colour from green chlorophyll, which absorbs the energy in sunlight. When the tree uses up all the chlorophyll, its leaves turn yellow and red.

Hide and seek

Hidden amongst the thick layers of rotting leaves, the woodcock uses its long bill to poke around for tiny animals to eat. With eyes positioned high on its head, it keeps a lookout for enemies at the same time.

Sticky tongue

At night, toads waddle from their dark shelters in search of insects, larvae, spiders, slugs, and worms to catch on their sticky tongues.

Snails have rough tongues to break off their food.

Insects make up 70 per cent of the animals in a deciduous forest.

Stripy forager
The striped skunk uses its long, sharp claws to dig into burrows and rotting wood for all sorts of food. If threatened, it aims a strong-smelling spray at its enemy.

A bed for the winter
During the autumn, the dormouse feasts on hazelnuts. As the weather becomes colder, it makes a nest of leaves and grass, then curls up to sleep until spring.

Soil from inside the tunnels gets piled up into molehills.

Underground tunnels
As the mole moves quickly through its maze of underground tunnels, it eats the earthworms and other animals that have fallen inside.

Forest fungi

Fungi play a vital role in a forest. They feed on dead plants and animals turning them into nutrients, which enrich the soil. Then, other plants soak up these nutrients to keep healthy.

The bright red colour warns that this fungus is poisonous.

Puff, puff!

To distribute its spores, the puffball puffs them out of a hole in its cap, like a cloud of smoke. The many millions of spores are then carried away by the wind.

Under the cap are the gills, which is where the spores are stored.

Partners

Some fungi, such as fly agaric, form a partnership with a tree nearby. They link up with the tree's roots and supply it with nutrients. The tree gives them moisture and food.

In the soil, there is the main part of the fungus – a maze of thin threads searching for food.

Deadly taste

The mushroom cap and stalk are the only parts of a fungus that can be seen. For people, the death cap is one of the most poisonous mushrooms in the world.

As it grows, the cap is joined to the stalk before it opens out.

The stalk base shows the remains of a veil that once protected the cap.

The bracket-shaped cap of the birch polypore becomes flatter and darker as it gets older.

The parasites

Often, a group of birch polypores attacks a living birch tree, feeding on it and draining it of its food supplies. Eventually they kill the tree and then continue to live there feeding on the dead wood.

In autumn, the mushroom, or fruit, of the fungus appears.

Forest words

Nutrients These are the minerals and other useful substances that plants need for growth and strength.

Parasite Something that feeds off another living thing.

Spores These are the tiny seeds of a fungus.

Winter journeys

Every year, almost half of all the world's birds travel from the forest where they breed in the summer to a warmer climate where they can feed in the winter. These flights, known as migration, are often long and dangerous, and they use up a huge amount of energy.

Spot the birdie

This spotted flycatcher is showing how it got its name. Some of its relatives spend their summers in Europe, then fly to Africa in the autumn. Others breed in North America, and travel to Central or South America for the winter.

Moving on

Honey buzzards (see below) are large birds that feed on the meat they get from hunting. They breed in the forests of Britain, but when winter comes, they fly all the way to Africa.

EUROPE

ASIA

AFRICA

Honey buzzard migration route

Coming home

Baby honey buzzards like to eat wasp larvae. There are lots of these in Britain's forests in May, so this is the time when the adults return from Africa to breed.

These babies grow up fast

Living the high life

Orioles spend most of their lives high up in the trees. Once in a while, they sweep down to the ground to splash in a lake or a pond, or to pick up nuts and insects to eat.

Golden orioles usually winter in Africa, but this one has left its European home to soak up the sun in Oman, near the Arabian Sea.

Spreading their wings

In September, the honey buzzard sets off again for Africa. These birds are adapted to flying long distances by having big wings and a long tail.

so they'll be able to fly south with their parents.

Travel options

Blue jays are found all across North America as far south as Texas. Some of them fly south in winter, but others stay where they are, storing food, such as nuts and acorns, to last them through the colder weather.

Migrating facts

● Arctic terns travel 35,000 km (21,000 miles) every year, from the Arctic to the Antarctic and back again.

● Before they set off, some small birds eat enough to double their weight. This extra fat gives them energy for their long journey.

Needles and cones

Forests in chilly climates are full of Christmassy trees, such as pines, spruces, and firs. Instead of papery leaves that drop off in the autumn, they have hard needles that stay on all year long. These trees are known as evergreens.

Male moose have huge antlers with up to 20 points on each one.

Giant deer

The largest member of the deer family – the moose – lives in coniferous forests. In the winter, it munches on tree bark, and sometimes eats so much from one tree that the tree dies.

Spiky rodent

The slow-moving porcupine can be found noisily chewing leaves and branches in trees, or on the forest floor. It can raise its many thousands of spiky quills when threatened.

Capercaillies are about the size of turkeys.

Dancing display

In the spring, the male capercaillies gather together and perform a dance to attract a female. They make a drum-roll, gurgling sound and leap around.

Hard case

Like this hardy spruce, most needle-leaf trees produce scaly cones that protect their seeds. This kind of tree is called a conifer.

Antlers are covered with smooth, furry skin that is known as "velvet".

Forest facts

● The dark green needles stay on so that they can start making food for the tree immediately the weather warms up.

● In dry weather, the scales on the cones open out and the seeds fall out.

● Little sunlight gets through the trees, so only small plants grow on the dark forest floor.

Cold killers

Hunting for food is a challenge in the cold, dark forests. The hungry predators have to cover large territories to find enough to eat. They have adopted fierce and clever techniques to track down and kill their prey.

Wolf facts

● Wolves are the largest members of the dog family.

● A wolf pack is led by a main male and his mate. This pair always eat from the prey first.

● A wolf pack eats almost every part of a carcass as they never know when their next big meal will be.

Pack hunters

Grey wolves work as a team to catch large animals, such as moose and caribou. Through scent, sound, and sight, they search for a weak animal. They then split into smaller groups to surround it and, when close enough, they all break into a run to catch it.

Air attack

The long-eared owl glides and hovers almost silently searching for small animals and birds to catch. It gets its name from the two tufts of feathers on its head, which are not ears at all.

Agile raider

Always hungry, the pine marten hunts for any small animal on the woodland floor, and has the agility to climb trees for raiding nests and catching tree-dwellers. Nuts and fruits are also part of its varied diet.

The glutton

The ferocious wolverine is named the 'glutton' due to its very large appetite. Although it's only the size of a small dog, t chases reindeer into snowdrifts and kills hem with a bite from its powerful jaws.

Frozen forest

During winter in the coniferous forests, the temperature can drop to below -40°C (-40°F). The ground is frozen hard and covered with snow. With very few hours of daylight, how do the plants and wildlife survive?

The waxy-coated needles and the downwards-slanting branches let the snow slide off without breaking them.

Forest retreat

In the winter, caribou move into forested areas to find food. They scrape the snow with their broad hooves to uncover the lichen.

Fur coat

Living only in the cold land of Siberia, the sable has thick fur to keep itself warm. However, people nearly hunted the sable to extinction for its coat.

Sharp-eyed

With keen eyesight, the northern goshawk perches on branches to watch for any bird or animal to catch. Its rounded wings and long tail allow it to fly swiftly between the trees. The goshawk moves from its territory when food is scarce.

The big sleep

Just before winter, black bears eat lots of food so they put on a thick layer of body fat. Then they find a cave, or den, where they can sleep during the very cold months. During this time, when food is not available, they can live off their fat.

ARCTIC TRAVELLERS

Reindeer is the name given to tame caribou that are owned by people living in the Arctic. The reindeer can be ridden, or used to pull sleds. Some are eaten and their hides are used for clothing. At the end of the winter, the herds leave the forests and head north for the summer. They can walk easily on the snow because their broad hooves spread out, acting like snowshoes. The people pack up and travel with them.

27

Suffocated forests

Large areas of conifer forests in Europe and North America are dying. Many scientists believe this is because air pollution coming from thousands of miles away is damaging the trees.

Burning fuels

Factories, power stations, and cars are all involved in the burning of petrol, oil, or coal. Whenever this happens, chemicals, such as sulphur and nitrogen, are released into the air.

Clouds are then swept over long distance

Action box

What can we do to help?

● Use less electricity by turning off lights, computers, and other electrical appliances when we are not using them.

● Only fill a kettle with the amount of water we need. Boiling a full kettle uses up more electricity.

● Use a car less by walking, cycling, sharing car trips, and using public transport.

Acid mix

Inside clouds, the chemicals join with water vapour and turn into acid. The clouds sweep across to the forests. Then the acids fall in rain or snow damaging the trees.

Liming the lakes

Animals and plants living in the lakes and rivers are killed by the acids. By pouring lime into the water, the lakes become less poisonous, so that fish and plants can survive.

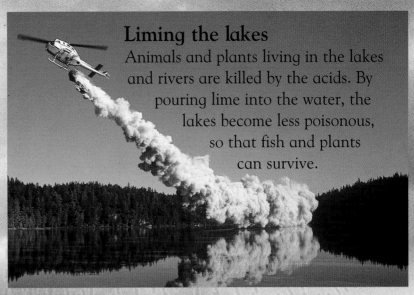

Acid attack

Acids damage the needles, so the trees cannot produce enough food to stay healthy. Pests and diseases can now attack more easily.

Poisoned trees

Acids also soak into the soil. Trees cannot grow well in the poisonous soil and eventually die. Even if air pollution is reduced dramatically, it would take many years for the damaged forests to recover.

to the coniferous forests by air currents.

Record breakers

Plants hold the records for being the world's biggest and oldest living things. Ancestors from one particular species have lived on Earth for over 150 million years. How have they achieved this?

Oldest living trees

On the dry, barren slopes of the White Mountains of California, USA, free from competition by other trees, are the aged bristlecone pines. One named "Methuselah" is 4,768 years old, and was a seedling when the Egyptian pyramids were being built.

Oldest species

The ginkgo family of trees grows throughout the world, and has survived for millions of years due to its resistance to disease and pests.

General Sherman

The largest living thing (by volume) is a giant sequoia tree named "General Sherman". It has a very, very thick trunk. Its total mass is estimated to be ten times more than a blue whale, and it is still growing!

Drive through

The towering redwoods thrive on the damp, rich soils of the Californian coastal forests. The tallest one is 111.25 m (365 ft) tall, which is about the size of an Apollo space rocket.

Under the canopy

From above, rainforests appear as a
vast green canopy, such as in the Amazon.
Underneath, plants are growing everywhere.
These forests are an amazing, colourful, and
noisy home for a wide variety of animals.

Jewel of the forest
Light on the wings of the blue
morpho reflect a stunning blue
colour. But, the wings' underside
is brown with eyespots, which
makes the butterfly hard to
see when it rests.

*Twisting around
the tall tree trunks
and branches are
fast-growing vines
called lianas.*

Thick rope-like creepers grow upwards towards the light.

Slow and steady
Moving slowly, the
unusual two-toed
sloth hangs upside-
down from branches
with its hook-like claws.
Its damp fur is covered by
algae and filled with insects.

Terror of the forest
Watching eagle-eyed from a lookout branch, the harpy eagle is the
biggest and strongest bird in the
rainforest. Its large gripping talons
can pull a sloth out of a tree.

Flashes of colour

In the canopy, colourful scarlet macaws fly around, filling the forests with screeching calls. They are only silent when eating.

The pools inside the bromeliads are home to more than 250 different animals, such as frogs and insects.

Air plants

Rooted in tree trunks, high above the ground, bromeliads flourish. Rainwater collects in the centre and this provides a drink for many animals.

33

Rainforest floor

Plants with large, shiny leaves, scented flowers, and tasty fruits, as well as dead leaves falling from the branches of trees high above, cover the ground in a rainforest. It's a busy place with much of the action hidden from our sight.

Buttress roots

A tangle of far-reaching roots spread out across the rainforest floor. The soil is thin and does not have much goodness. So, the roots grow out from the trunks to support the tall trees and soak up much-needed nutrients near the soil's surface.

Ant eaters

A tamandua uses its sharp front claws to open up ant nests, and then puts a long, sticky tongue inside to lick up the ants. It does not destroy the nests, so that it can return another time.

Pollinator

Feeding at night, the fast-flying, long-tongued bat visits strongly scented flowers. The flower's pollen falls onto the bat and gets passed to the next flower the bat visits.

This bat has a long, narrow tongue to drink the nectar inside the flower.

Big squeeze

Curled up in low branches, the world's heaviest snake, the anaconda, rests for days after a large meal. It kills by wrapping its powerful body around its prey and squeezing until the animal can't breathe. Anacondas swallow their victims whole, headfirst.

Night-time meals

Scampering along a system of paths, this paca (a small rodent) sniffs out fruits and leaf buds in the dark. Pacas shelter in burrows or hollow trees during the day.

Leaf cutters

Busy leaf-cutter ants cut out pieces of leaves and carry them over their heads to their underground nests. The fungus that grows on the chewed leaves is food for the ants.

WORLD'S STRONGEST

Rainforests are home to over 30 million species of insects. Some insects, such as the rhinoceros beetle, play a very important part in recycling the nutrients in rotting wood and leaves back into the soil for use by living plants. While humans can carry only about three times their body weight, rhinoceros beetles can carry an amazing 850 times their own weight. They get their name from the horn on their head, which they use for fighting rivals, digging, and climbing.

Getting around

The dense rainforests are like large adventure playgrounds with so many plants for climbing up, scrambling over, swinging across, or jumping from. But the animals are not necessarily playing.

Leaping lemurs

With speed, lemurs can leap from trees to escape from enemies. They hold their bodies upright as they jump so that their hands and feet are ready to grip the next tree trunk.

Lemurs use their powerful hind legs to spring from trees.

Prowlers

The jaguar's spotted coat breaks up its outline amongst the plants on the forest floor. Camouflaged, it quietly prowls around searching for animals to eat. It can even climb low branches to catch monkeys.

Cautious climber

At night, the slow-moving pottos awake to search for food trying to avoid being seen by predators. It places one strong gripping foot in front of another as if walking on a tightrope.

Gliders

Active at night, the colugo has a thin, furry layer of skin stretching from its fingers to its tail. It spreads this out as it glides from tree to tree in search of plants to eat.

Swingers

In the forests of Borneo and North Sumatra, orang-utans can be found living in the trees. Their very long arms, which span up to 2.5 m (8 ft), are ideal for swinging from branch to branch.

Young orang-utans stay with their mothers for up to ten years learning from them.

Up in the clouds

Most tropical rainforests lie in low places, such as river valleys. However, some of them grow so high up on mountains that they are in the middle of a cloud all the time. This special damp environment is home to lots of rare animals and plants.

Mountain monkey

Pileated gibbons are small apes that live in the Cardamom Mountain forests of Thailand. Bit by bit, the trees are being cleared, so the gibbons face extinction.

Nosy parker

At home in New Guinea's mountain forests, the long-beaked echidna is one of the few mammals that lays eggs. The nose that gives this creature its name can be up to 20 cm (8 in) long.

Living together

The cloud forest of Malaysia is one of the last sites in the world where Asian elephants, rhinos, and tigers all live in the same place. Asian elephants have much smaller ears than their African cousins.

Brilliant plumage

Gripping onto a branch with its small feet, this resplendent quetzal displays its shimmering colours high up in the branches of the Costa Rican cloud forest. Only the male birds have these exotic feathers.

Gorillas in the mist

The cloud forest of central Africa is one of the few places mountain gorillas are found. Conservationists work hard to keep their habitat safe and protect them from hunters.

NATURE'S NURSERY

Many of the plants that grow in cloud forests cannot be found anywhere else. In the mountain forests of Peru, for example, there are thought to be more than 1,000 species of rare orchid. One small area alone contains more different types of plant than are found on the whole continent of Europe.

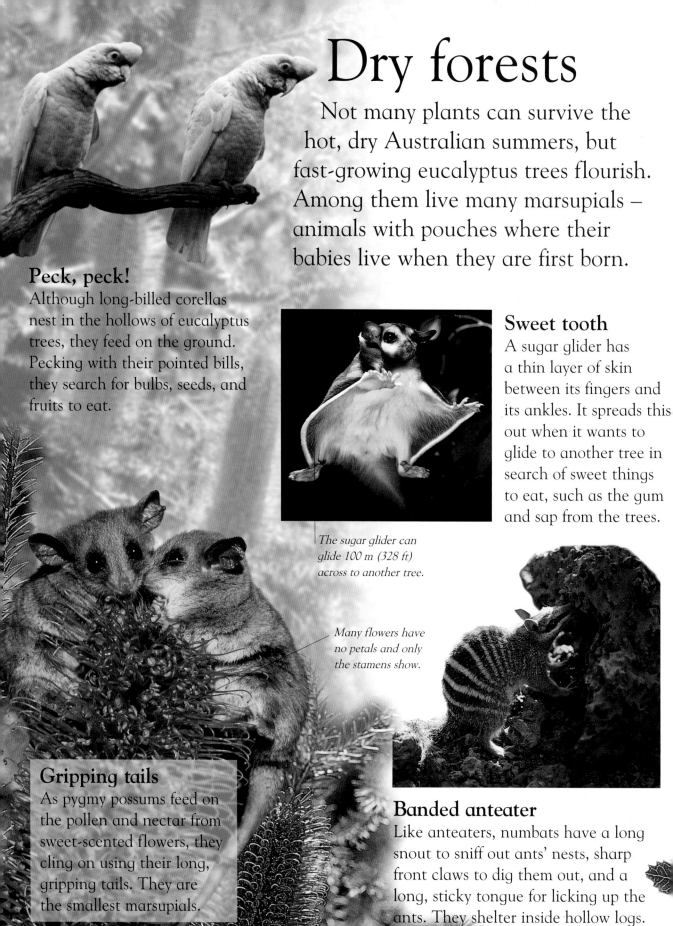

Dry forests

Not many plants can survive the hot, dry Australian summers, but fast-growing eucalyptus trees flourish. Among them live many marsupials – animals with pouches where their babies live when they are first born.

Peck, peck!

Although long-billed corellas nest in the hollows of eucalyptus trees, they feed on the ground. Pecking with their pointed bills, they search for bulbs, seeds, and fruits to eat.

Sweet tooth

A sugar glider has a thin layer of skin between its fingers and its ankles. It spreads this out when it wants to glide to another tree in search of sweet things to eat, such as the gum and sap from the trees.

The sugar glider can glide 100 m (328 ft) across to another tree.

Many flowers have no petals and only the stamens show.

Gripping tails

As pygmy possums feed on the pollen and nectar from sweet-scented flowers, they cling on using their long, gripping tails. They are the smallest marsupials.

Banded anteater

Like anteaters, numbats have a long snout to sniff out ants' nests, sharp front claws to dig them out, and a long, sticky tongue for licking up the ants. They shelter inside hollow logs.

The evergreen eucalyptus leaves have a tough coating that stops water loss.

Little devil

Tasmanian devils are so named because they have a loud screech and fierce looks, and now live only in Tasmania. Their favourite food is dead animals.

"No drink"

Koala is an Aboriginal word meaning "no drink". The cuddly-looking koala feeds entirely on eucalyptus leaves and gets enough water from them. Often it spends 80 per cent of its day asleep.

Waratah

The large, dome-shaped flowerheads of the waratah shrub are made up of hundreds of small flowers. The bright colours attract birds to feed on the nectar the flower produces.

Forest fires

Fires can help forests to recycle goodness in dead plants and to clear the way for new growth. However, if a forest fire gets out of control then it can cause lots of damage.

Raining buckets

Helicopters dip large buckets into nearby lakes to scoop up large amounts of water, which are then released over the fire. Within minutes, the helicopters can be back with another load.

Fighting fires

On the ground, firefighters try to stop the fire from spreading. They cut down trees to make a gap called a firebreak.

Goggles prevent sparks flying into the eyes.

Fireproof clothing protects the firefighters from the heat.

Axes and chainsaws are used to chop down trees.

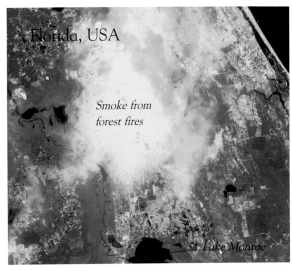

Florida, USA

*Smoke from
forest fires*

Lake Monroe

Cooling the fire

Firefighting planes called airtankers are used to pour thousands of litres of fire retardant over the flames. The retardant is a red-dyed liquid, which slows down and cools a fire.

Fire watch

Space satellites can help firefighters by producing infrared pictures of big blazes. On this one, which shows part of the US state of Florida, smoke is blue, plants are red, ground is green or brown, buildings are blue or grey, and water is jet black.

Some fir trees need a fire's heat to release their seeds.

Preventing fires

When camping, always take extra care using fire, such as

- storing flammable liquid containers in a safe place,

- never taking burning sticks out of a fire,

- always checking that the campfire is out when leaving.

New life

In amongst the burnt remains of a forest, new seedlings soon appear. They grow quickly with little competition, more sunlight, and renewed goodness in the soil.

Survival of the forest

All over the world, forests are being destroyed. Some trees are cut down for their wood, but often it's their land that is wanted for farms, buildings, or industry. In some places, though, disappearing forests are slowly being replaced.

Forest facts

- If we keep destroying rainforests at this rate, they will all be gone in 100 years.

- When trees are cleared, the soil around them gets washed away, leaving barren land.

Cultivation

The Brazilian rainforest is one of the world's most famous endangered habitats. Here, a great chunk of it has been cleared to provide commercial farmland.

Giant problem

Over the last few decades, the Chinese forest habitat of the giant panda has shrunk by 50 per cent. Threatened with extinction, this creature has become a world symbol of conservation.

LAST-MINUTE SAVE

Butterflies of all kinds are threatened by the destruction of their forest habitat. During the 20th century, for example, the numbers of Schaus swallowtail butterflies in Florida, USA, fell so low that they nearly became extinct. To save them, a large conservation programme was launched, and today their population is growing and thriving.

Taking care

Once new trees are planted, trained conservationists keep watch to make sure they are growing normally, and they stay free from pests and diseases.

Damage repair

To replace forests destroyed years ago, these Sri Lankan children are planting tree seedlings they have grown themselves on the hills near their village.

New for old

Some forests are designed to be replanted as soon as they are cut down. These are known as sustainable forests. Here, new seedlings are well protected so they can grow as tall as the trees around them.

Forests are very precious – find a tree to love today!

How can I help?

Paper is made from trees, so try not to waste it, and recycle as much as you can to help keep our future forests safe.

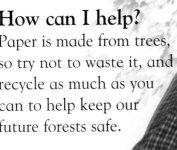

Glossary

Here are the meanings of some words it is useful to know when you are learning about trees and forests.

Acorn the smooth, hard fruit of the oak tree.

Algae simple plants without roots, stems, or leaves, which usually grow in water.

Bark tough protective layer on the outside of a tree's trunk and branches.

Bromeliad a type of epiphyte that has a rosette of stiff leaves at the top where rainwater collects.

Bud small bump that turns into a flower, a leaf, or a stem.

Burr a fruit or seed with a prickly or sticky covering.

Buttress root a root that grows from a stem or trunk, near the soil's surface.

Carbon dioxide colourless gas absorbed from the atmosphere by plants.

Camouflage colour or pattern that blends a plant or animal into its surroundings.

Chlorophyll the green chemical in plants that uses the Sun's warmth and light.

Climate the average weather of an area in terms of rain, wind, temperature, etc.

Cone the fruit of a coniferous tree. Cones have scales on the outside to protect their seeds.

Coniferous having cones to hold seeds instead of flowers and fruits. Coniferous trees have needles instead of leaves.

Conservation the process of saving plants and animals from damage and destruction.

Deciduous having leaves that drop off in autumn, and grow again in spring.

Diet the food and liquid that a particular animal eats.

Drey squirrel's nest. Dreys, which are about the size of a football, are lined with leaves.

Epiphyte a plant that grows on another plant, but does not use its food or water.

Evergreen having permanent leaves or needles.

Extinct plant or animal species that has died out.

Fern simple plant; one of the first to grow on Earth.

Fertile (soil) rich in the nutrients plants need to grow.

Firebreak strip of bare land intended to stop a fire.

Flower the part of a plant responsible for reproduction.

Fruit the part of a plant that contains its seeds.

Lichens low-growing plants found on hard surfaces like rocks, trees, and bare ground.

Migration moving from one place to another to find food or warmth.

Nectar sweet liquid inside flowers that attracts insects.

Needles long, hard, needle-shaped leaves usually found on conifer trees.

Nut hard, dry fruit with one large seed inside.

Nutrients "foods" that plants and animals need to stay healthy.

Parasite plant or animal that takes its nutrients from another living thing.

Petrified (trees) preserved by minerals dissolved in water.

Photosynthesis the way plants use water, carbon dioxide, and sunlight to produce food.

Pollen powder produced by flowers for use in reproduction.

Pollution harmful gases and particles in the air.

Predator an animal that kills other animals for food.

Prey an animal hunted by other animals for food.

Rainforest dense forest that grows in hot, wet climates.

Root the part of a plant that absorbs and stores food and water from the earth.

Seed case containing the tiny beginnings of a new plant, and enough food to help it start growing.

Seedling young plant that has grown from a seed.

Sett badger's underground home, or burrow.

Species group of living things that have characteristics in common, and can breed with one another.

Spore tough case containing a tiny collection of cells that can produce a new plant.

Sustainable (forest) designed to be replanted when it is cut.

Temperate a climate that is never very hot or very cold.

Tropics the hot regions on either side of the Equator.

Trunk the main stem of a tree, which supports its roots and branches.

Index

Acknowledgements

Dorling Kindersley would like to thank:
Janet Allis for original illustrations; Sarah Mills and Gemma Woodward for picture library services; Jacqueline Gooden and Laura Roberts for design assistance.

Picture credits

The publisher would like to thank the following for their kind permission to reproduce their photographs:
a=above; c=centre; b=below; l=left; r=right; t=top;

Alamy Images: Jim Nicholson 8cr; Alan Wheeler 41background, **Ardea London Ltd:** 36cl; Ian Beams 17tr; Jean-Paul Ferrero 40crb, 44bl; Masahiro Iijima 27tr; Jaime Plaza Van Roon 41br, **Bruce Coleman Ltd:** Bruce Coleman Inc 32-33; Marie Read 21bl; **Corbis:** Chris Beddall/Papilio 17br; Niall Benvie 11; D Boone 42bl; Andrew Brown 10tl; Andrew Brown/Ecoscene 6clb; Mike Buxton/Papilio 14bc; Gary W Carter 15tl; Ralph A Clevenger, W Cody 7tl, 22cla;W Perry Conway 10cl, 15bc, 27l; D Robert & Lorri Franz 24bl; Michael and Patrica Fogden 38-39; Gaetano 45tl; Raymond Gehman 42bc; Collart Herve/Sygma 35tl; Dave G Houser 43bc; Wolfgang Kaehler 35br; Galen Rowell 30bc; Gary Joe McDonald 7tc, 24bc; Gunter Marx

Photography 23cla; Massimo/Mastrorillo 28tl; Robert Y Ono 22bc; Michael Pole 4tl; J M Roberts 42cb; Sanford/Angliolo 2br; Walter Schmid 6cla; Kennan Ward 39tl; Randy Wells 46-47; Tony Wharton,/FLPA 19tr; Terry Whittaker/FLPA 35clb, **DK Picture Library:** 16bc; Brian Cosgrove 28-29; Natural History Museum 5crb, 6cb, 14ca; Richmond Park; Alan Watson 7cr; Jerry Young 7cr, 6bl, **FLPA - Images of nature:** Frans Lanting 44ca, **Nature Picture Library Ltd:** Martin Dohn 28bc; Hanne and Jens Eriksen 21tr; Jeff Foott 8crb; Jorma Luhta 22bl; Dietmar Nill 24-25, 35ca; Premaphotos 12bc; Jeremy Walker 8tl, **N.H.P.A.:** ANT 40ca; G I Bernard 45clb; Stephen Dalton 18tl; Manfred Daneggar 25cr; J Dennis 36ca; Martin Harvey 38tl; Daniel Heuclin 36bc; Robert Erwin 15tr; Pavel German 38cra; T Kitchen & V Hurst 17cla, 25cl; Mike Lane 42tr; Eero Murtomaici 20bc; Dr Ivan Polunin 37tl; Andy Rouse 13cla, 36-37; Jany Sauvanet 32br; Kevin Schafer 39tr; Roger Tidman 17cla; WLD 33cla, **Oxford Scientific Films:** ER Degginger/AA 12cla; Breck Kent 30-31; Stan Osolinski 38clb; Richard Packwood 29bc; Alan Root 34bc; **Popperfoto:** 43bl. **Lynn Rogers:** 1, 27bc; **RSPB Images:** Paul Doherty 21c, **Science Photo Library:** Earth Satellite Corporation 43tr, **Still Pictures:** Mark Edwards 29tr, 45tr; Klien/Hubert 41tl; Dani/Jeske 31bc; Bruno Pambour 29tl; Roland Seitre 33br; Jean-Claude Teyssier 10cr; **Getty Images:** Laurie Campbell 13crb; Angelo Cavalli 18-19; Daniel J Cox 26; Howie Garber 40tl; Kevin Schafer 34; Gary Randall 12-13; Lori Adamski-Peek 45br.

All other images © Dorling Kindersley
For further information see: www.dkimages.com